Dementia of Love

Olga Sandoval

BookLeaf Publishing
India | USA | UK

Presentation by *BookLeaf Publishing*

Web: www.bookleafpub.com

E-mail: info@bookleafpub.com

ISBN: 9789358316452

First edition 2024

DEDICATION

Mom

A gloomy night

In the sky,

I looked at a star.

It smiled at me,

and I responded to it.

She said that my steps

have been taken care of since birth.

I love her

and am so grateful

to love her like this.

She is a unique and perfect lady

synonymous with a great achiever.

She has been my mother until now.

I don't know what her destiny is

or how far together it will take us,

but me being your daughter,

Mother you will be until eternity.

It is,

and you will be,

the most sacred thing that life gives me

my happiness.

I know

I will not have enough life

to thank you, MOM.

- Tu hija, Corazón de Poeta

ACKNOWLEDGEMENT

As I reflect upon the completion of this journey, I am filled with overwhelming gratitude to God, the Supreme King, the guiding force that has illuminated my path and granted me strength throughout this endeavor.

To my beloved mother, Rosa Eva Mejia, whose sacrifices and encouragement have shaped me into the person I am today, I am eternally thankful.

To my cherished children - Robert, Michelle, and Alvaro - you are the heartbeat of my existence. Without your presence and unwavering belief in me, I could not have dared to be the protagonist of my own life story. Your love has been the fuel that propelled me toward realizing my dreams.

A special acknowledgment is reserved for my daughter, Rita Michelle. Your dedication to translating "Dementia de Amor" from Spanish to English bridged language gaps and transcended the boundaries of our shared passion.

To all those who have played a role, no matter how small, in bringing this project to fruition, thank you.

With profound appreciation,
Olga, Corazón de Poeta

PREFACE

Dementia of Love is a book written with
delicacy, with words deriving from a heart
brimming with love or lack of love, so that you,
my dear reader, can identify with these poems
written with stories, lived or told. Ultimately,
these are stories that either you or I have lived or
will live. By reading my poems in verse or
prose, we will be accomplices and take our
imagination to another level with poems
pleasing to the senses. This small work ends at
the age of 65, where the experience of life is
what predominates. I hope, my dear readers, that
reading me inspires each of you so that the art of
reading and writing never dies.

Sunrise

Sunrise
that radiates tranquility
Breeze
that brings peace to my being
a poem full of love
a silent "I love you" with your sweet voice.
Without caring about autumn,
we melt with love
making them one,
the immensity of the Universe
clothing us.

I nestle into your chest,
enjoying the fragrance of your skin,
seeing how the butterflies flutter and dance,
emanating heat within our bodies, enjoying us to
the fullest.

The singing of the birds that snuck in behind our
window,
welcoming the new day,
announcing a pleasant awakening that surprised
us in flagrante,
overflowing with happiness.

- Olga, Corazón de Poeta

Today

Today
I die of love
at the whim of fate
that insisted on leaving me alone,
unable to see beyond my eyes,
sacrificing my freedom and happiness.
What a lack of self-love.

Today
I will sail against the current,
showing myself what I am capable of,
of that and much more.

Today
with a broken and empty heart
I say goodbye to you.

Today
my love is translucent and clear,
to sweeten my life.
I have no more ties.

Today
I am free to love.

- Olga, Corazón de Poeta

Confession

Before you,
I wanted to touch the sky
and now,
I have been living there since I saw you arrive.

You have sweetness and perversion in your eyes,
I fall in love with you more at sunrise.
That look of your soul reflected in your eyes,
it is the door of your heart where love resides.
You'll realize I don't need guitars or violins
to tell you that, within me,
that is where you live.

I have even fallen in love with your intellect
like a storybook from a fairytale,
my body is enveloped with love.

I don't think expressing your love
to the one you love the most
is corny or a sin.
It would be a sin to stay silent
and let everything in the past remain.

Today, I confess that I love you.
I need you by my side,

I am not to blame for loving you.
It is your fault
for having what I desire.

- Olga, Corazón de Poeta

It is You

My best smile
my shelter, strength and hope
my best poem
it is you
who makes me dream
and makes my eyes shine
a total elixir
it is you
who makes my hair stand on end
and drives my senses crazy
who rubs my heated skin
it is you
my yesterday, my now and my tomorrow
the Sun that gives warmth to my body
the Moon that illuminates my path
my shelter, my joy and my happiness
it is you.

- Olga, Corazón de Poeta

Subtle Desire

I made a wish to the night,
And you arrived.
I made a wish to the Moon,
And you arrived.
I made a wish for my life,
And you arrived.
Today, my best poem is YOU.

- Olga, Corazón de Poeta

A Child's Heart

My Child's Heart is still here,
next to me, no matter the passing of the years,
despite the harm that some of them may have
caused.
I continue learning about life and living from
dreams.

I know that love is enjoyed,
that sometimes you suffer,
and I cry like a helpless child,
but I continue to treasure my childish Heart.

I thank my soul that whispers to me every
morning
that I am strong,
whispering to me
to not weaken,
to smile for my triumphs,
to amend my mistakes,
to sing, live, dream and embrace the joy of
having
A Child's Heart

- Olga, Corazón de Poeta

Save Me

Save my kisses on your lips,
save me in a space within your thoughts,
but save me, especially in your heart.
Save me in your memories
in the secret torrents
that your rivers carry,
in the wisp of air and the silence of my poetry.
Save me in every pore of your skin,
without rush or time,
that way, I will think that I live to love you.

- Olga, Corazón de Poeta

Withered Rose

Oh, the damage you must have suffered
to now, see you near oblivion
your sad face, your pale cheeks
your petals completely withered by the Sun.

How many sleepless nights
you must have had,
in your gloomy home
your cry almost lost
in this abandoned and empty garden.

Your gaze is absent
under a gray sky without your presence,
without anyone looking for you or missing you.
You have been forgotten
odorless and colorless.

Today, only cold, distance, and darkness
they accompany you,
sad eyes and weakened hopes,
how sad to see you so defeated and surrendered.
I can only sadly say "goodbye" to you.

- Olga, Corazón de Poeta

Here I Am

My heart raced when he said,
"Here I am to caress each of your marks of life,
to appreciate your gray hair one by one,
and to make you smile.
Here I am to give you freedom,
to accept your ideas,
to admire your skills,
and to share your happiness.
Here I am to support you at every moment,
to accept your flaws,
to celebrate your virtues,
and to especially accompany you to fly with
your wings,
to love you,
and to receive the same from you."

At my age, that made me soar.

- Olga, Corazón de Poeta

Sea, Sun and Water

Here I am
admiring nature
and telling the sea my
feelings,
today, I throw them into the waves
to free my thoughts.

I will toss away your kisses that once took me to
glory.
Today, they have become history,
along with the caresses that made me fly,
those that you didn't know how to value.

The aroma that you left impregnated in my body,
all the promises and dreams shared, until today...
they have only caused me harm.

Sea, Sun, and Water
they are witnesses of this confusing love,
so many tears that I shed for you
but today...
the waves washed my face,
the Sun took care of drying them
and this way...
I say goodbye to you.

- Olga, Corazón de Poeta

Indifference

One day, I will walk on the flowery path
where every pain caused by
contempt and indifference are forgotten,
leaving only the experience that life leaves
behind.

I will pluck your rooted memory, and
everything will pass into oblivion.
It's silly to stumble several times,
but it's sillier not to have lived them.

This world is that of madmen,
we overthink and feel too little,
dreams that sadden our souls.
Today, I will look toward Heaven
without believing that I still love you.

- Olga, Corazón de Poeta

Habits

I grew so used to you
that today,
my soul, alone and wild,
calls out your name.
I feel you here.

The distant sea resonates
and a seagull departs from dawn.
My body tires from thinking of you,.
and you so far away.

Something rises to my eager mouth
I madly vibrate with electric efforts
that intoxicate me with you,
I close my eyes, and you disappear
into spirals of smoke.

That summer night
is forever engraved in me.
My voice breaks, and my body fills
with nostalgia and hopelessness.

- Olga, Corazón de Poeta

Enough

15

And I loved him until my mind and heart
shouted,
"Enough!"
Just like you came into my life,
little by little, you left me,
your perfume on my skin.
Today, it tastes bitter.

I thought that one day,
you would be my perfect complement.
Oh, how sorry I am.
Today, I know that what I needed was to find
myself.
I have finally achieved it,
you will only be part of my past
because, everything about you,
I have forgotten.

- Olga, Corazón de Poeta

My Prayer

I beg the night not to lie to me
and the rain not to deceive me.
I want to drink your waters
and navigate in your gaze.

I beg the Moon not to lie to me
and the Sun not to deceive me.
I want to burn from you,
lose myself in your body
and squeeze your soul.

I beg the sea not to lie to me
and the sand not to deceive me.
I want to wrap you
in the waves of the calm sea
and bathe in you.

I beg time not to lie to me
and your body not to deceive me
I want to be prey to your thoughts
and your hands,
living in the sweetness of your gaze.

Perfect and desired supplications,
you and I

confined in time
exploring the Universe, forever united
Heart to Heart.

- Olga, Corazón de Poeta

Somber Winter

This winter's rain bathed my soul,
and the harmonious breeze gladdened my being.
I remembered the sweetness of your frenetic
kisses,
those kisses that transported me to a different
world.

Today, when I remember them,
these verses of love emerge
that in my soul I have kept for you,
verses that make my smile fly free
in the landscape of passion.

- Olga, Corazón de Poeta

Envelop Me

You came to me
when I needed it most,
you awakened in me
the most noble and beautiful of feelings.

A lady also expresses her feelings,
says, "I love you,"
"I need you,"
and it propels you to soar.

Love me today
burn my heart
love me in a thousand ways.
Love me unconditionally.

Envelop me with fantasies,
with a sweet heat that burns my heart.
Let me rest in your lap with true, transparent
love
that beautifies, blooms, and quenches my thirst
to love you.

- Olga, Corazón de Poeta

Longevity

When the years go by
and you are no longer the same
with your longevous gaze and nullified mobility
falling into an abyss.

When the only thing remaining is
the memory of an old love song
of those past loves,
the unforeseen pranks,
a story between clouds of cotton.

Then, you will know that
life was a sigh
and you will arrive
where you have never been.
You bought that train ticket in vain
because it's already on its way out.

Hope is there,
love is brief
and oblivion is so great.

- Olga, Corazón de Poeta

Dementia

In vain, I insisted on dressing in your memories,
I wanted to flood my life with passion
with torrents of clear water,
with hopes that one day
you would turn what I felt into bubbles of
fantasies,
but they were failed illusions.

You took me through endless waves of emotions
enveloping me in an open sea,
sometimes confusing,
sometimes serene,
sometimes agitated
causing an unfathomable noise
that became more uncertainty
of a disturbed memory
and a Dementia of Love.

- Olga, Corazón de Poeta

Beauty

Beautiful faces
are those that reveal
in their countenance
the light of a pleasant soul.

Beautiful hands
are those that perform
kind and noble acts.

Beautiful feet
are those that rush
to alleviate the pain of others.

Beautiful words
are those that come
from a grateful heart,
those that motivate
and lift the spirits
of those who read or listen to them.

Beautiful ears
are those that listen to you.

A beautiful person
is the one who witnesses

your tears fall
and with a word of encouragement
revives you
and gives you peace.

- Olga, Corazón de Poeta

Dreams

In the silence,
I cry out your name.
I hug the pillow to calm my loneliness.
There, confused, I find peace and tranquility.
A pleasant perfume caresses me.

I close my eyes, and in my dreams, I see you.
I repaint my dreams of fantasies.
My thoughts are filled with melancholy
and I lose myself in the deep ocean of your eyes,
believing to find you
on the shore of my Heart.

- Olga, Corazón de Poeta

Goodbye

With hands of silk,
he caressed my cheeks.
Tears flowed from his eyes.
Sad and sobbing, he said, "Goodbye,"
his gaze lost to infinity.
In his eyes, I could see his sadness
with a silent voice, he whispered, "I love you"
and said goodbye.

I grasped his hands
I looked him in the eyes
I kissed his lips
and I told him…"Wait for me in the afterlife."

Loneliness came over me
a deep pain in my heart
I told him, "My life you take with you."

Today, neither tears nor breath remains for me.

- Olga, Corazón de Poeta

Printed in the USA
CPSIA information can be obtained
at www.ICGtesting.com
CBHW071008130424
6870CB00042B/791